MH-53E SEA DRAGONS

BY DENNY VON FINN

BELLWETHER MEDIA · MINNEAPOLIS, MN

EPIC

EPIC BOOKS are no ordinary books. They burst with intense action, high-speed heroics, and shadows of the unknown. Are you ready for an Epic adventure?

This edition first published in 2014 by Bellwether Media, Inc.

No part of this publication may be reproduced in whole or in part without written permission of the publisher. For information regarding permission, write to Bellwether Media, Inc., Attention: Permissions Department, 5357 Penn Avenue South, Minneapolis, MN 55419.

Library of Congress Cataloging-in-Publication Data

Von Finn, Denny.
  MH-53E Sea Dragons / by Denny Von Finn.
    pages cm. – (Epic: Military Vehicles)
  Audience: Ages 7-12.
  Includes bibliographical references and index.
  Summary: "Engaging images accompany information about MH-53E Sea Dragons. The combination of high-interest subject matter and light text is intended for students in grades 2 through 7"– Provided by publisher.
  ISBN 978-1-62617-081-0 (hardcover : alk. paper)
  1. Sikorsky H-53 (Military transport helicopter)–Juvenile works. I. Title.
  UG1232.T72V64 2014
  623.74'6047–dc23
                        2013036769

Printed in the United States of America, North Mankato, MN.

The photographs in this book are reproduced through the courtesy of the United States Department of Defense. A special thanks to the following for additional photos: Ted Carlson/ Fotodynamics, p. 14; Svitlana Kazachek, p. 9.

TABLE OF CONTENTS

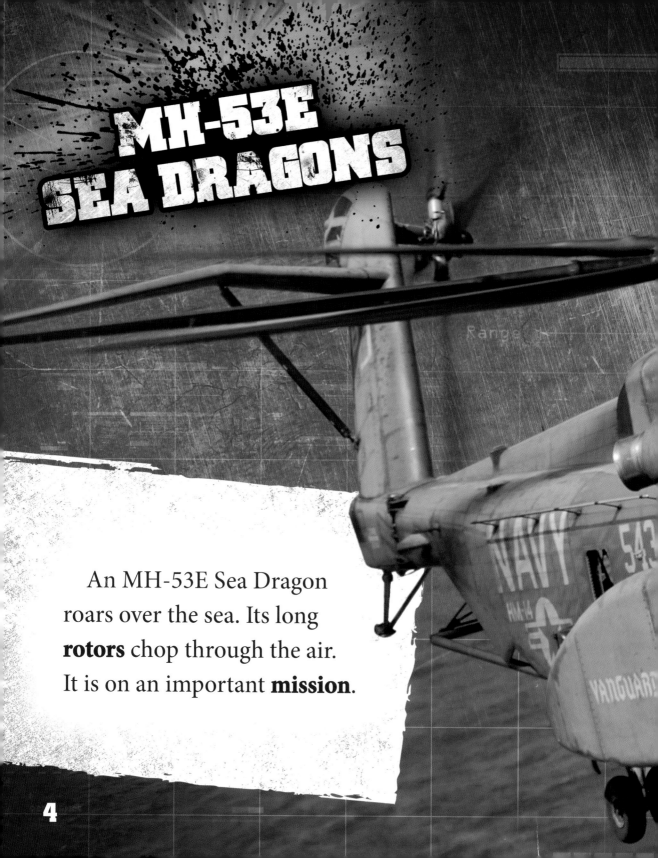

MH-53E SEA DRAGONS

An MH-53E Sea Dragon roars over the sea. Its long **rotors** chop through the air. It is on an important **mission**.

Latitude > 44° 49' 6" N

Longitude > 2°°

Level

ROTOR

543

Two pilots fly the Sea Dragon. Their crew searches for **mines** in the water. Mines are a danger to U.S. ships.

BLACKHAWKS

Sea Dragon Fact

The Sea Dragon can reach a speed of 173 miles (278 kilometers) per hour.

COUNTERMEASURE

The crew attaches a cable to a **countermeasure** on the water below. The Sea Dragon pulls the countermeasure over the mines. The mines explode. The sea is now safe for Navy ships.

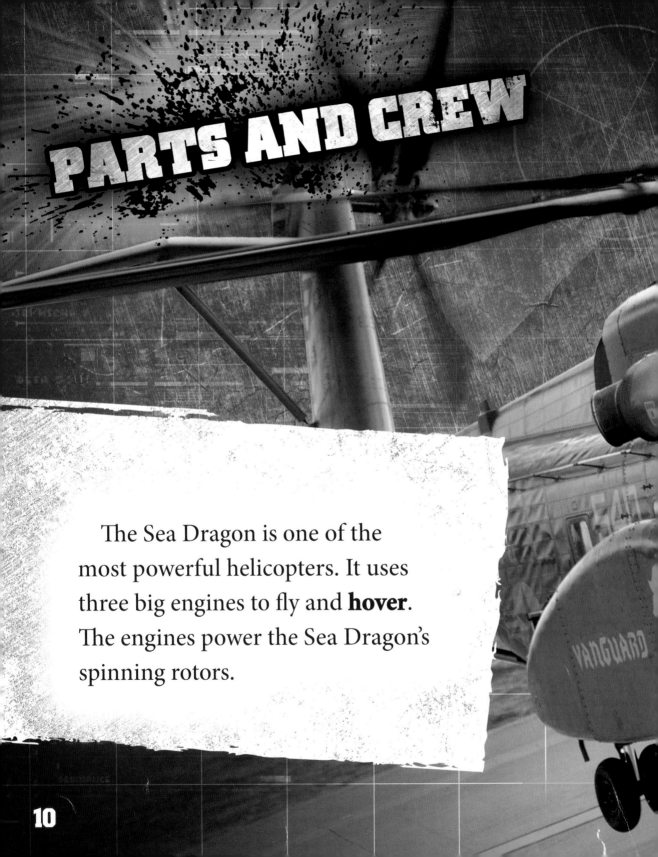

PARTS AND CREW

The Sea Dragon is one of the most powerful helicopters. It uses three big engines to fly and **hover**. The engines power the Sea Dragon's spinning rotors.

ENGINES

SPONSONS

Sea Dragon Fact

A Sea Dragon can be refueled in the air.

Sea Dragons sometimes have to fly very far. They have large **sponsons** on each side. These carry extra fuel.

The pilots sit in the Sea Dragon's **cockpit**. Large windows let them see the sky above and the sea below.

PILOTS

COCKPIT

02

SEA DRAGON MISSIONS

The Sea Dragon's main mission is **minesweeping**. It drags countermeasures across water to clear mines.

Sea Dragons also deliver **cargo**. They move supplies to **aircraft carriers** at sea. Sometimes they bring food to people affected by floods and other disasters.

Sea Dragon Fact

The Sea Dragon can lift almost twice its weight!

VEHICLE BREAKDOWN: MH-53E SEA DRAGON

Used By:	U.S. Navy
Entered Service:	1986
Length:	73.3 feet (22.3 meters)
Height:	28.3 feet (8.6 meters)
Weight:	69,750 pounds (31,638 kilograms)
Rotor Diameter:	79 feet (24 meters)
Top Speed:	173 miles (278 kilometers) per hour
Range:	1,208 miles (1,944 kilometers)
Ceiling:	10,000 feet (3,048 meters)
Crew:	3 or more
Weapon:	machine gun on some
Missions:	minesweeping, cargo delivery

Sea Dragons are some of the world's largest helicopters. These big aircraft and their brave crews are ready to help wherever they are needed.

GLOSSARY

aircraft carriers—large ships that airplanes and helicopters can take off from and land on

cargo—supplies that are moved by a vehicle

cockpit—the area of an aircraft where the crew sits

countermeasure—a large, floating device that a Sea Dragon pulls across the sea to explode mines

hover—to stay in one place above the ground

mines—devices that float in the water and explode when ships sail over them

minesweeping—a military mission that clears the sea of mines

mission—a military task

rotors—the spinning parts of a helicopter; a Sea Dragon has a top rotor and a tail rotor.

sponsons—tanks attached to an aircraft to hold extra fuel; a Sea Dragon has two sponsons.

TO LEARN MORE

At the Library

Abramovitz, Melissa. *Military Helicopters*. Mankato, Minn.: Capstone Press, 2012.

Alvarez, Carlos. *MH-53E Sea Dragons*. Minneapolis, Minn.: Bellwether Media, 2011.

Harasymiw, Mark. *Military Helicopters*. New York, N.Y.: Gareth Stevens Pub., 2013.

On the Web

Learning more about MH-53E Sea Dragons is as easy as 1, 2, 3.

1. Go to www.factsurfer.com.

2. Enter "MH-53E Sea Dragons" into the search box.

3. Click the "Surf" button and you will see a list of related Web sites.

With factsurfer.com, finding more information is just a click away.

INDEX